Little Book of Real Estate for Sellers & Buyers

by

Linda Stalvey

Acknowledgements

I'd like to thank my husband for his unwavering support whenever I decide to go off on another path…and there have been several over the years.

A special shout out to Jean Mannarino, the Realtor who lost a client and gained a colleague. We had been looking at a house with Jean, when she said, "You know more about this house than I do. Have you ever thought of becoming a Realtor"? My husband and I cracked up laughing. After our first house sale fell due to agent neglect, I swore I would always know what the market was doing wherever I lived. Real estate became a passionate avocation. I even had a mantra: "In my next life, I'm going to be a Realtor." Thanks to Jean, real estate is now a passionate vocation and I don't have to wait for my next life.

Jean had also said, "My manager would love you." When I sat down with Karen Thompson, I knew my real estate home would be in her Howard Hanna Office. She has been a tremendous mentor, support and 24-hour guide. I told her I'd be in the business as long as I was having fun. Still having fun!

Cheers to my long-time writer buddy, editor and all-around gal pal, Pam Frost. She has the technical ability I don't, and without her this book would still be a Word doc on my computer.

And finally, to the Realtors and clients who may find this Little Book of Real Estate a useful tool in helping to create successful transactions, my sincere gratitude.

Part One

LITTLE BOOK OF REAL ESTATE FOR SELLERS

Part Two

LITTLE BOOK OF REAL ESTATE FOR BUYERS

Begins on page 28

Part One

LITTLE BOOK OF REAL ESTATE FOR SELLERS

So, you're thinking about selling your house.

Prepare for the experience of a lifetime. Whether it is a good experience or a bad experience will depend, for the most part, on you—your attitude, expectations and choices. Even if you've sold a house before, every real estate transaction is unique.

Many proceed without a hitch. Some will encounter hiccups. And, some transactions will die.

To help you manage whatever comes your way, this little book will offer information on the transaction processes, hints to move through them with less stress, and an inspirational quote, affirmation and prayer, as either a first or last resort depending on your belief system.

Let's start the process.

"I long, as does every human being, to be at home wherever I find myself."
Maya Angelou

God, grant me the serenity to accept the things I cannot change, courage to change the things I can, and wisdom to know the difference.

I am guided to make the right decisions in the right time to move forward.

YOU ONLY HAVE ONE CHANCE TO MAKE A GOOD FIRST IMPRESSION

If you have the luxury of time, you can actually have fun and make money prepping your house for sale. If time is not yours, there are still many things you can do to help assure a faster sale.

If you remember nothing else, remember this: CLEAN AND DECLUTTERED SELLS!

Let's start with the first part of this maxim: CLEAN.

The first picture a potential buyer will see is one of the front of your house. Can the front of your house be seen or is it covered by overgrown shrubbery? Is your front door clean and porch inviting? Fresh paint may be in order for door and shutters. If so, please consult an expert for color choices. Is the lawn trimmed and edged? Are there appropriate pops of seasonal color? Is the roof and siding free of algae, mold or moss? Is the concrete in good repair? Are play items or trash cans put away and unused yard equipment and recreational items disposed of?

Clean and decluttered applies inside and out. If that first picture is not pleasing, the buyer will flip to the next listing and may not even see the wood floors and stainless-steel appliances inside.

When that buyer does walk into your house, he or she gets an overall impression before looking at detail. Little things can make a big difference like clean baseboards, vents, fans, appliances, windows, sills and tracks, carpeting, and grout between tile for starters.

If you don't have the time or inclination to perform the deep cleaning necessary, please contract with a cleaning company to have it done. It will be worth the investment.

Once your house is clean, keep it that way!

Don't underestimate the power of fresh, neutral paint and professionally cleaned carpet. It's probably your biggest bang for the buck.

It's not always necessary to put the latest kitchen counter in, or paint your cabinets the latest popular color or reface to a different wood. Remember: CLEAN SELLS.

Decluttering

Professional Stagers use something called the 70 Percent/30 Percent Rule when it comes to decluttering and it's a good rule to follow. When you live in a house, 70 percent of what is in a room is comprised of your "things" and 30 percent is the space in the room. The percentage flips when you are on the market. Seventy percent of each room is space and 30 percent is filled with your "things." Remember, you are selling your house, not your things. *Every inch of space you declutter is money in your pocket in equity.*

"Things" can and should include furniture. From personal experience I can tell you when you reach that

30 percent mark, you will feel uncomfortable in your own home. Hurray! It's not your *home* anymore. It's a *house* and you are caretaking it for the next owner. (and yes, you can get the box of tissues because it is not an easy process)

Many Realtors take staging classes and/or hold certifications as Realtor Staging Consultants. Ask your Realtor for assistance for there are several other staging rules that can make a difference in selling your house.

When decluttering and staging it helps to think of packing…every knick-knack, decorative item or picture you pack now is one less you or your mover has to pack when deadlines might be tighter than you'd like.

Storage units can become your friend. Too much furniture, too many toys, too many clothes, too many holiday decorations. You get the picture. The 70/30 rule applies in storage areas like closets and basements too.

A special word on closets. I'm sure you've heard that we tend to use 20 percent of the clothes in our closets. Try winnowing down to those clothes when on the market, especially if your house isn't blessed with large double walk-in closets in the master and walk in closets in other bedrooms.

Another option is to use the Japanese art of folding clothes. More clothes in a drawer look neater if you must go with quantity. Check You Tube for Marie Kondo Folding Method videos.

What you don't need, sell. There are many online, newspaper and Facebook options to do so. Save the money you make in selling the old, for buying new for your next house. Motivation doesn't hurt.

There are some things you may choose to give to family or friends. Other items you may want to donate to a local non-profit. All are good options for they get unused/unwanted things out of the house and out of the landfill.

Again, please remember, you are selling the space in your house—not your things.

A special word about wallpaper. For many potential buyers, wallpaper is a deal killer especially if all your walls are covered in the '80s or '90s finest patterns. Taking paper down and painting in a neutral palette should help to sell your house faster and at a higher price.

In decluttering and staging the goal is to appeal to the broadest number of people. Thus, your agent may suggest that while you love that purple master bedroom, it might appeal to more people if it were a neutral gray or beige. Your stenciled phrases in every room may not appeal to the masses. Do not take it personally. Your house is a commodity to sell.

TAKE A BREATH ...
AND CHOOSE ONE OR MORE OF THE
FOLLOWING FOR INSPIRATION

"Clutter in your physical surroundings will clutter your mind and spirit." Kaniesha.com

Lord, give me the strength I need to face today's cleaning and decluttering tasks. It may be daunting and I may not enjoy the never-ending cycle, but I can express gratitude for the end result whether by my hand or the hands of others. You have given me the gift of shelter. Let me express my gratitude with pride in my environment.

Cleaning and decluttering is a process of letting go of the old to make way for the new.

FOR SALE BY OWNER
OR SELL WITH A BROKER/AGENT?

If you want to guaranty a higher stress level, try selling your house yourself. It's much more than planting a For Sale sign, getting on the internet and waiting for a buyer to show up. The process is complicated at best. Legal requirements change frequently and unless you are adept at decluttering, staging, preparing the proper property disclosures, pricing, writing an attractive house description, photography, marketing, advertising and holding open houses, negotiating with agents and buyers, establishing legally binding dates for loans, inspections and inspectors for your general home inspection, point of sale, radon, mold, pest, well, septic, or specialized inspection, closings and filings, dealing with loan officers, escrow and title companies, writing escrow letters, dealing with low appraisals and working with your buyer and/or buyer's agent DON'T SELL BY YOURSELF....YOU WILL NOT SAVE MONEY, IT WILL TAKE YOU LONGER, AND YOU WILL DRIVE YOURSELF CRAZY.

Leave the crazy part to the professionals who thrive on that environment, are up to date on the latest legal requirements and are there for you in a fiduciary relationship.

A fiduciary relationship is one of trust and confidence in which one party [your Realtor] *owes* the other [the seller(s)--YOU] loyalty and a higher standard of good faith than they owe to third parties [the buyer(s)]. The duties of the fiduciary are: accountability, confidentiality, care, obedience, loyalty, and disclosure. Your lawyer or limited service broker will not provide a fiduciary relationship. Your Realtor will!

"Anyone can put you on the right path but they can't make you walk it, you have to make that first step and decide if you're on the road to success or failure." Rashida Rowe

Loving Spirit, you have blessed me with many talents. Bless me with the knowledge to know when a task is not mine to do. Help me find a professional to sell my house who will communicate honestly with me, perhaps even telling me things I'd rather not hear. Bring me a talented, enthusiastic Realtor who will relate to me in a manner in which I am most comfortable. I, in turn, will respond with honesty and enthusiasm and together we will place that sold sign on this property.

I will enter into a relationship with a Realtor who best fits my needs and personality.

IT'S NOT JUST THE COMMISSION....
REALLY!

Brokers (the real estate company) are not created equal. Neither are agents. When picking a broker and/or agent to sell your house, look at programs and marketing plans the company and/or agent will use to sell your house. The savings come in moving your house off the market quickly so you can stop paying taxes, utilities, insurances and mortgages on a house you no longer wish to live in. This is especially important if the house you are selling is vacant.

You will be entering into a relationship with an agent to handle perhaps one of the largest monetary transactions you will make. It pays to interview more than one agent and comparison shop. Working with an agent is like working with a massage therapist—you want someone you like and trust who has the appropriate skill set to get the job done.

Is there a difference between a real estate sales agent and a Realtor? Yes, there is! A Realtor is a member of the National Association of Realtors. Realtors have continuing education requirements including classes in ethics, law and fair housing, and

Realtors abide by a Code of Ethics. Ask if your agent is a member of the National Association of Realtors.

Questions you might ask:

- What is the market share of the broker? In other words, how many houses, or those on the market, does a real estate company sell?
- What are the statistics for internet traffic on broker website? Will your listing be syndicated on other websites?
- Will the broker target direct mail marketing?
- Will the broker advertise in newspapers?
- Are there opportunities for TV advertising?
- Is there a 100% Money Back Guarantee offered to buyers?
- Is the broker's office open seven days a week?
- Is there an automatic option for home searches?
- Is there a relocation department?
- Are there affiliated businesses with the broker like mortgage, home warranty, title or insurance services? If so, does agent receive financial compensation from those service companies?
- Is the broker/agent experienced with new home sales?
- What is the agent's experience? Have they received any sales awards? Are they a Realtor and member of the National

Association of Realtors and thus abide by a Code of Ethics?

- What is the agent's 30-day marketing plan for your house?
- How does your agent network within and without the brokerage?
- Will the agent meet the appraiser with a packet of good comparables?

Back to those commissions. Please realize your agent does not get the entire commission! Each commission is split four ways with half the pie going to the listing broker and half the pie to the selling broker. The agent on each side of the sale gets a percentage of that initial split, often starting at 50 percent. If you ask your agent to reduce his or her commission you might want to consider what part of his or her job description you would like to barter.

"In this world, you get what you pay for." Kurt Vonnegut Jr.

Caring Spirit, life is always requiring decisions. When a new opportunity presents itself, I may feel unsteady and unsure of which way to go. I may feel unsettled about making a decision, especially when there is still some fogginess in my heart about the course I should take. Please guide my thoughts. Help me be patient, and help me trust the spirit of intuition you have given me as an aid for recognizing the signs that help me move forward. I know your boundless grace will bring goodness to the decision I make. Thank you for your love and guidance. Amen.

I will interview more than one Realtor and make my decision based on my left- brain analysis, how I feel with this person, and my intuition or "gut feel" trusting I will know the right person.

THE LISTING CONTRACT

The first question (or second if commission is first) is, "What's my house worth?"

That depends a lot on you! Have you done a thorough job of cleaning, decluttering and making minor repairs?

Your Realtor will evaluate your house and compare it with similar houses currently on the market or recently sold in your neighborhood. This analysis is called the CMA or Comparative Market Analysis. He or she will suggest a range for pricing the house or suggest a list price. The final decision on price always lies with you, the seller.

Your Realtor will explain why getting the price right from the beginning is critical to the sale of your house. Your first two or three weeks on the market will garner the most attention. If you price too high thinking you can always come down, you may lose potential buyers. If you are just "testing the market" because you "don't really have to move," you are racking up days on the market leading a potential buyer to wonder if something is wrong with the house.

If you "need to get x amount of money out of your house" the market may not agree with you.

Remember, your Realtor does not establish the sale price. You don't either. The sale price is decided by the real estate market. Sale prices, unless cash offers, must also appraise for the sale price. More about appraisals later.

Now that your house and yard are ready, and you've talked about pricing and how your house will be advertised, it's time to get the listing contract signed.

Read all the fine print and make sure you have a copy of this legally binding document. This is one of the biggest transactions you will make, make it knowingly. A good Realtor will explain in detail what you are signing.

How long is your listing contract? A year is common, but shorter increments, like six or nine months can also be negotiated.

Can you cancel the contract if you are not happy with the broker/agent? If so, how is that accomplished?

Are you liable for commission if you get a sale and the sale falls?

Many real estate brokers offer home warranties which can be written to cover both seller and buyer. Many of today's buyers are looking for the home warranty. Protect yourself and help make your house more attractive to the buyer. Consider adding a home warranty to your listing contract. The cost of the home warranty is generally taken off proceeds of the sale at closing.

Property Disclosures are part of the listing contract. Your Realtor will provide you with the appropriate disclosures for your property. Please be totally honest when filling them out. To do any less is to ask for problems in the future.

If you are in a Home Owner's Association or Condominium Association you may be filling out additional forms for those too.

With the paperwork done, your agent will either shoot pictures of your house or have a professional photographer do so. Your hard work in cleaning and decluttering will pay off in the photos. Drone photos are becoming popular. You may want to ask your Realtor if drone photos will be taken or if they are necessary in your market.

Showing criteria will also be established. How much time will you need to be ready for a showing? Requests to show may come in at any time of day. Do you need to have the children or dog taken out of the house by you or a sitter? Do you work? The more you can make your house available to show the better it is.

There is no hard and fast rule about how many showings result in an offer to purchase. Some houses go quickly and some linger on the market. Sometimes remedies are apparent, others, like location cannot be changed.

During the time you are on the market, take care of yourself and family and take care of your house. It can be a stressful time if you let it be so.

"Nobody can go back and start a new beginning, but anyone can start today and make a new ending." Maria Robinson

God, we thank you for the roof over our head. We thank you for giving us our home. We need to pass it off into other hands now. We ask for your blessing in this process. Bring us together with the right buyer, someone who will enjoy being nurtured and supported by this house. Play matchmaker, Father. Give us wisdom to make any changes in the house itself or in our expectation of price to bring this about. Give us creativity to look outside the box and to think of new possibilities. We trust you with this transaction and know that all is in Divine Order.

As every door closes another opens, although it may be challenging in the hallway. I know everything is working out for my good.

ON THE MARKET

Your Realtor only has control of advertising your house.

You, the seller, have control over pricing and the condition of the house.

Location cannot be changed.

Open Houses

Will your agent offer open houses and how frequently? How will open houses be advertised? You may hear that open houses are only good for the agent. NOT SO! Many houses are sold at open houses. Yes, your agent may get another client from your open house. Why would this be a problem? You have someone to promote your house, someone who knows the most about your house, chatting with potential buyers for a set period of time.

You also may have heard that the only people who show up at Open Houses are nosey neighbors. This is also a myth. Yes, your neighbors might walk through your house, it's human nature! Your neighbors also know a lot of people, some of whom may be interested in buying your house. Let them see it so they can talk about it!

Please take care to keep medications, guns and valuables locked away. As a safety precaution, a Realtor generally will not leave the first floor of the house, nor will they follow visitors through your house. If you have a very large house, it might be appropriate to have more than one person host the Open House, but generally, trust your professional to do his or her job as they see fit.

Your Realtor will review comments received about your house at private showings and open houses. This can be great information to tweak your house to make it more attractive buyers.

Leave the personality behind and accept this critique at face value.

TAKE A BREATH …
AND CHOOSE ONE OR MORE OF THE
FOLLOWING FOR INSPIRATION

""If you don't like something change it; if you can't change it, change the way you think about it." Mary Engelbreit

Make my heart ready to say goodbye. Make my heart also ready to say hello. Open my soul to accept a new place and new things, New people, new opportunities, and new challenges. Bless my move, those involved in the process, and this adventure.

I open my house to its new owners.

YOU HAVE AN OFFER!
IS IT A CONTRACT?

Sooner or later you will receive an offer. Now the fun begins.

It's time to negotiate!

It's not always the highest offer that makes the best offer. You want a qualified buyer with an excellent chance of making it to close and title transfer. Information your agent will review with you about that offer will include the following:

- Agency—who is working for whom.
- What is the price of the offer?
- Is it cash or financed?
- If financed, does the buyer have a solid pre-approval?
- Is the buyer's loan conventional, FHA or VA?
- Is the buyer asking for seller concessions/assistance with purchase?
- What inspections are ordered?
- When does the buyer want to close?
- When does the buyer want possession of the house?

- Will the buyer allow you to stay in the house after title transfer? Will there be a cost attached?
- Are there multiple offers?
- Is the buyer asking for any of your furnishings or yard equipment?

Once you evaluate the offer, you may accept the offer, counter the offer or decide not to proceed at all. Even if you receive a lowball offer, it pays to respond. There are many reasons a buyer may start low, for instance it may be a cultural issue, the buyer likes to negotiate, or perhaps the buyer is a flipper who wants to make quick money. You just don't know.

You Have a Contract!

Once the negotiations are completed and the purchase offer is signed and delivered to the buyer's agent and buyer, you are under contract. The dates in your contract are legally binding and must be met. Dates include when your buyer will make a formal loan application and when that loan will be approved, inspections, walk through, and close and title transfer. Your agent will be very busy during this time ensuring that critical dates are met, and that all the concurrent processes that go into a sale are proceeding accordingly.

There are three critical areas for a seller to be aware of: financing, appraisal, and inspections. Each of these processes presents a possibility for re-negotiation or worst-case scenario, the contract falls.

Financing is simple. Your buyer does something to no longer qualify for the loan, such as buying a new car, changing jobs or experiencing a life change.

Appraisal. The bank financing your buyer's loan will have an appraiser evaluate the house. A good Realtor will have a packet of information prepared to help make the appraiser's job easier. This packet will include comparable sales to support the sale price, a list of recent improvements to the property, and a plat.

A low appraisal will open negotiations. Possible outcomes include the buyer putting down more cash, the seller reducing the sale price to appraisal price, meeting somewhere in the middle or the sale falls.

Inspections can also open negotiations. After the inspections, the buyer may come to the seller with a list of contingencies—I will continue with the sale if you fix _______________. Perhaps the radon test showed radon levels over the legal limit and the buyer is asking you, the seller, to install a mitigation system. That can be costly. Or perhaps the electrical box needs some attention…perhaps not so expensive.

Your Realtor will guide you through the process.

Once the contingencies are released, the transaction proceeds to close. Both parties sign the legal documents to transfer ownership, release liens and payoff old and install new mortgages. Monies are sent to appropriate parties and the title is transferred in the local courthouse.

YOU SOLD YOUR HOUSE!
CONGRATULATIONS!
Call your mover!

TAKE A BREATH …
AND CHOOSE ONE OR MORE OF THE
FOLLOWING FOR INSPIRATION

"And suddenly you know…It's time to start something new and trust the magic of beginnings." Meister Eckhart

 Thank you, God.

 It is all good. Gratitude all around.

Part Two

LITTLE BOOK OF REAL ESTATE
FOR BUYERS

Congratulations! You've decided to buy a house.

Prepare for the experience of a lifetime!

Whether that is a good experience or a bad one will depend, for the most part, on you—your attitude, expectations and choices. Even if you've bought a house before, every real estate transaction is unique. Many proceed without a hitch. Some will encounter hiccups. And, some transactions will die.

To help you manage whatever comes your way, this little book will offer information on the transaction processes, hints to move through them with less stress, and affirmations, inspirational quotes and prayer as either a first or last resort depending on your belief system.

Let's start the process.

TAKE A BREATH ...
AND CHOOSE ONE OR MORE OF THE
FOLLOWING FOR INSPIRATION.

"I long, as does every human being, to be at home wherever I find myself." Maya Angelou

God, grant me the serenity to accept the things I cannot change, Courage to change the things I can, and wisdom to know the difference.

I am guided to make the right decisions in the right time to move forward to my (our) next perfect home.

REALTOR VS. GOING IT ALONE

With a major investment ahead, one of the first questions a buyer has is, "What will it cost to have a real estate professional represent me?"

The good news is the big commissions are paid by the seller. Many brokers will charge the buyer client a modest commission, usually in the $200-$300 range to represent you in a transaction.

The broker is the real estate company whose signs you see around the neighborhood. Each broker has agents who work as broker representatives in helping you find a house and guiding you through the transaction. These individuals may be a sales agent or a Realtor. The terms are related, but not interchangeable.

A Realtor (rhymes with doctor), is a member of the National Association of Realtors. As such, each Realtor has continuing education requirements to maintain including courses in ethics, law and fair housing. Each abides by a Code of Ethics.

Your Realtor enters into a fiduciary relationship with you. A fiduciary relationship is one of trust and confidence in which one party [your Realtor] *owes* the other [the buyer(s)--YOU] loyalty and a higher standard of good faith than they owe to third parties [the seller(s).] The duties of the fiduciary are: accountability, confidentiality, care, obedience, loyalty, and disclosure.

Going it alone is fraught with pitfalls. Unless you are an expert in establishing your price point, searching for houses—often times in a competitive market, negotiating with a seller, or seller and Realtor, establishing legally binding dates for loans, inspections [such as your general home inspection, point of sale, radon, mold, pest, well, septic, or specialized inspection] closings and filings, dealing with loan officers, escrow and title companies, writing escrow letters, dealing with appraisals you want to work with a Realtor.

Your lawyer or limited service broker will not provide this level of service. It is well worth the small amount of commission charged to work with a Realtor.

Searching for a new house can be challenging. When choosing to work with a Realtor, remember you are entering a relationship which may include some amount of stress. Choose someone with whom you are comfortable, can communicate with freely, and who has the credentials you feel will best serve you. Real estate credentials can look like alphabet soup. If your Realtor doesn't explain the significance, please ask for an explanation.

Your Realtor may ask you to sign an Exclusive Buyers Representation Agreement. He or she will be devoting a good deal of time and effort to help you find the perfect house. As they are committing to you, your Realtor would appreciate the same commitment from you. These agreements can be signed for two or three months. This allows both parties time to see if they can work well together, and gives each the option of renewing the agreement or "divorcing" if they cannot.

Unlike many other professions, your Realtor doesn't receive a paycheck unless you buy a new house. If you don't get keys, your Realtor doesn't get paid.

A word about real estate commissions. Please realize your Realtor does not get the entire commission. Each commission is split four ways with half the pie going to the listing broker and half the pie going to the selling broker. The agent/Realtor on each side of the sale gets a percentage of that initial split, often starting at 50 percent.

You may want to interview Realtors and compare services. Some brokers are "one stop shopping" where you can secure a mortgage, insurance, warranty, and title services if you choose. This can provide a level of ease during a transaction if all the players are "in house."

Some Realtors receive compensation for using in house services. If so, they must disclose that relationship to the buyer. Ultimately, it is the buyer's choice if and where to obtain those services.

Once you've chosen your Realtor the fun starts. You are one step closer to a new house!

"Be genuinely interested in everyone you meet and everyone you meet will be genuinely interested in you" — **Rasheed Ogunlaru**

Be at peace. Do not look forward in fear to the changes and chances of this life. Rather, look to them with full confidence that, as they arise, God, to whom you belong will in His love enable you to profit by them. He has guided you thus far in life, and He will lead you safely through all trials.
St. Francis de Sales

I look forward to the excitement of finding a new house. I look forward to moving into a new home.

Step 1 – The Pre-Approval

The first question your Realtor will ask is, "Do you have a mortgage pre-approval?"

Please ignore this section if you are a cash buyer. The cash buyer will need to provide proof of funds. If you are not a cash buyer, please read on.

A pre-approval is not to be confused with a pre-qualification. And some lenders are blurring the lines between the two. A good mortgage pre-approval will not only check your credit scores, but will insist on documentation to assess your financial well-being. Basic documents commonly needed for a pre-approval include the following:

- Prior two year's tax returns and W-2's (all addendums)
- Your most recent 30-day pay stub(s) showing year-to-date earnings
- Two months current bank statements for checking, savings and investment accounts (all pages)

You may be able to get an "instant" response from an online lender, but will you have the opportunity to ask questions and review terms and fees in detail? The online lender may give you an approval, but do you know what program you have been approved for? How much of a down payment the loan requires? Will you need seller assistance to close?

You will know the answer to questions such as these if you take the time to sit down with a lender who will educate you and answer questions. Comparison shop! You would do so if you were buying a car. Your house is much more of an investment over a longer period of time. Become an educated consumer. It's not always the lowest rate that provides the most savings!

Once you have a good mortgage pre-approval within a defined program you and your Realtor know the price point at which you can buy. There is no need to look at houses out of your approval range…as much fun as that might be.

If you have secured a pre-approval for a VA or FHA loan, your Realtor will ensure that he or she only shows you houses that will accept that type of financing.

Another reason to have a solid mortgage pre-approval is that it gives you a competitive edge in placing an offer on a house. When you finally find *the* house, you don't want financing standing in the way of seller acceptance of your offer.

Start the process with a competitive edge. Shop for your mortgage and get a good pre-approval!

" When you think about it, three of our biggest financial decisions in life are made at times of peak emotional excitement: deciding to get married, buying a home, and having kids." Richard Kiyosaki

Thank You for Your Word, Lord God. Thank You for its message of truth and encouragement. I am especially encouraged today by the apostle John's words that reflect Your fatherly love: "I pray that you may prosper in all things." Give me the courage, Lord, to be a faithful steward of all that You have entrusted to me. Enable me to wisely untangle current financial knots. Most of all, even as I address today's financial needs, help me to look beyond them, to walk in Your truth, and to rejoice in the hope of eternity with You

I've done my homework. I am making a wise financial decision.

LOOKING FOR YOUR NEW HOUSE

You have your Realtor. You have your pre-approval. Now it's time to define what type of house will best serve you and/or your family. It's rare that a house will be exactly what you want. Generally, there will be a give and take. If you've watched any HGTV, you already know sometimes one must "go a little further out" to stretch your mortgage dollar. If school system is a primary concern, your Realtor can delineate a search within school boundaries. As you start looking at various houses, you may refine your criteria.

A word about working with your Realtor in the house search. Credit for real estate sales is a bit like capture the flag. Please contact your Realtor if you want to see a For Sale By Owner house; a house listed by another brokerage/agent; a house you've seen online, a house you've seen advertised on social media or in the paper, a house you've always liked but is not for sale.

When you go to an open house, please take your Realtor's business card with you and let the hosting agent know you are already represented. Your Realtor is working hard for you—let him or her do the talking and showing arrangements for you. To do otherwise may actually jeopardize your Realtor getting credit for your sale and making an offer and contract more complicated than it need be.

New House vs. Resale

New homes are generally more expensive per square foot. Builders will tell you they can build exactly what you want—and a custom builder can do just that. Production builders, the large common name builders, will offer you a selection of options...but they are not unlimited. If you are interested in looking at new builds, please let your Realtor know and he or she will be happy to accompany you to the builder of your choice. Your Realtor can help you negotiate with the new home builder. Yes, they do negotiate to varying degrees.

Why buy resale? The answer may be in landscaping, hardscaping, water features, lighting, and outbuildings among others that are often extras in a new build. A resale has moved through the new home warranty period where construction "bugs" may appear. And, established neighborhoods don't deal with construction traffic and value is fairly well established.

It might be financially advantageous to update a kitchen in a well-established neighborhood, put in new flooring or add new paint. A little bit of personalization may be all that resale needs to be your perfect house.

Since many people are updating and remodeling homes today, your chances of finding a home that is exactly what you want are also quite possible.

Showings

Depending on your time frame and housing inventory, you could be visiting several houses in one day, or visiting a few as they come to market.

Many homes will have showing restrictions requiring prior notice to show. This can vary from a couple of hours to a full day. Time is of the essence in real estate. Try to be flexible and let your Realtor know as soon as you see something you might like to visit. By the same token, if you are in a very competitive market or interested in a type of house that can potentially draw multiple offers, and your Realtor calls, you will not want to waste any time getting in to see the property.

In this age of high technology, it is wise to refrain from discussing features of a house while you are inside the house. That goes for positive or negative features. With recording devices readily available the last thing you want your seller to hear is what you think of the house or list price. Alexa and her cousins can put you at a distinct negotiating disadvantage.

As you look for your next house, it's wise to set up a system for notes. After visiting four or five properties it's easy for features run together. "Was that the house with the nice bathroom or funky kitchen?" If your Realtor provides the listing sheets, you can always make notes on the back and rank each house you've visited with a simple scale.

Whether you look at one house or 101 houses, pay attention to your gut feeling. There is often something palpable when you walk through the doorway of your next home, even if it's just a "feeling" that you can't rationalize.

Whether you look at one house or 101 houses, don't give up hope. There is a house for everyone!

"You will get there when you are meant to get there and not one moment sooner. So, relax, breathe, and be patient." KushAndWizdom

Heavenly Father, you can see me, you know me, and You know my needs. Father, my housing situation needs to change. I ask You to guide me to the right house, the house that will be best for all aspects of my life and the lives of my family and all others involved. I know You already have a place chosen for me—one that will be the best possible solution for me and all my loved ones. I thank you for that.

As I explore possible houses, I keep an open mind and an open heart.

THIS IS THE ONE!!!!!

Your search has ended. You've found the house for you! Now to prepare your offer and hope the seller likes it enough to accept it or counter it.

The contract may vary state-to-state but may have the following common components.

<u>Agency Disclosure</u>: This document identifies who is working for whom. It will name your agent and brokerage and the seller's agent and brokerage.

<u>Purchase Agreement</u>. There are several sections to this document. First, the property will be described and the offer detailed. Then dates will be established for financing, inspections, closing and title transfer, and possession of the house. These are legally binding dates. If they cannot be met, it will be necessary to add an addendum to remain in contract.

There is detailed information on how the transaction will proceed with respect to inspections and inspection contingencies. Acknowledgement of receipt of property disclosures and buyer responsibility toward the same is also part of the offer.

Additionally, buyer and seller costs and prorations are detailed in the purchase agreement. If a home warranty is purchased that will be noted.

Earnest money and dispute resolution is detailed. Disclaimers and damages are also addressed.

These are the major areas of a purchase offer. There are others as well. Ensure that you read all the lines in the document and have your Realtor answer any questions. It is a legally binding document.

Once signed, it will be transmitted to the seller's agent for presentation to the seller along with your pre-approval letter or proof of funds and earnest money check or promissory note.

Depending on the situation, you might also want to consider submitting a letter to the seller detailing why you want the house. Sometimes it's not the biggest offer that is accepted, but rather the offer from the family which has the same type of dog as the seller, or child with the same name as their grandchild, or some other type of personal or emotional connection.

Some agents will place a time limit on the offer. This can be a double-edged sword. Ask your Realtor to explain the pluses and minuses of such a restriction to the offer.

There are three possible outcomes to a purchase offer: the seller accepts your offer, the seller rejects your offer, or the seller counters your offer. If the seller counters, then it's game on. You and your Realtor will discuss strategy and decide how to proceed.

If this offer doesn't work out, you will go through the same process again until it does.

For the purpose of this book, let's say it does and extend congratulations.

"During a negotiation, it would be wise not the take anything personally. If you leave personalities out of it, you will be able to see opportunities more objectively." Brian Koslow

Lord, help me to remember that nothing is going to happen to me today that you and I can't handle.

I have a contract for a new house. May the transaction proceed seamlessly until the title is in my name.

THE PITFALLS THAT MAY KILL A SALES CONTRACT

Processes will proceed at a pretty fast clip from here until close and title transfer. Your Realtor will be working with a multitude of people to make sure the transaction moves forward as detailed in the sales contract. He or she will also be in steady contact to make sure you do all the things on your plate.

The first task for you will be to make a formal mortgage loan application.

Concurrently, you will be scheduling your inspections. Please choose a qualified inspector. Uncle Joe, the contractor, may be a good guy and know his stuff, but if he tells you there is something wrong with the electrical system and you ask the seller to repair, the seller doesn't have to do so because the "inspector" was not a licensed electrician or qualified inspector. The American Society of Home Inspection [ASHI] members are well respected and always a good choice. Your Realtor will be happy to provide referrals.

Your title company will forward paperwork to you for review and signature. Please be prompt in answering any communications from your title company.

Your inspections generally must be completed within 8-10 days after acceptance of the offer. If there are health or safety issues identified, you can ask the seller to remedy the issues. Your Realtor will prepare an amendment outlining contingencies to the sale. This may also open up negotiations. Inspections are a common place for a sales contract to fall.

Within two to three weeks, you should have the appraisal back, if financing the house. If the appraisal value is equal to or greater than the sale price, no further action will be necessary.

If the appraisal comes in low, it will be an opportunity to negotiate. The possible outcomes are:

- The seller reduces the sale price to the appraised value.
- You come up with more of a down payment to make up the difference.
- You and the seller split the difference.
- The contract falls.

The last common place for a sales contract to fall is in financing. Your mortgage lender will advise you to purchase NOTHING but essentials until after the house closes. It doesn't matter how qualified you are for the mortgage! Unfortunately, it's been known to happen that a buyer will get so excited about the new house that he buys new appliances, furniture, maybe a new car...and he no longer qualifies for a loan and his new house disappears in sales receipts.

Once you are through these major steps, it should be pretty smooth sailing to close and title transfer…unless the title company discovers an issue.

When your Realtor hears the magic words, "clear to close," you are within a few days of having new house keys.

Somewhere in the whirlwind of the above processes, you will have transferred utilities, packed, secured a mover, and filed change of address notices.

Finally! You have signed the papers and the title has transferred. There is nothing better than receiving keys and opening the door to your new home!

Just remember to change the locks.

TAKE A BREATH ...
AND CHOOSE ONE OR ALL OF THE
FOLLOWING FOR INSPIRATION.

"There is something permanent and something extremely profound, in owning a home. Kenny Guinn

 THANK YOU, GOD!

Today it's a house. Tomorrow it will be a home.

ABOUT THE AUTHOR

Linda Stalvey is a native of Parma Heights, Ohio who escaped the state after college and swore never to return. After a successful government career dotted with awards and recognitions, including one from Congress for an issue of the NIH Record (National Institutes of Health) that she conceived, developed and wrote, Linda took an early out retirement to become a full-time mom to daughter Brynn and part-time massage therapist.

Never say never! Linda returned to Ohio in 2005. She met Pam Frost shortly after while writing her first book, Dragon Dreams, a middle grade fantasy (available on Amazon print and digital or through the author for personalization). Without Pam, neither book would exist!

After meeting Jean Mannarino, Linda started her career as a realtor. She has alphabet soup credentials, writes excellent house descriptions and has been recognized with several sales awards.

Linda now knows why she is back in Ohio and feels blessed to be back home. Ohio has nurtured her passions, took her out of her comfort zone to try new endeavors, and added to her circle of friends. She never anticipated writing one book let alone two books. Perhaps there is a third lurking in the recesses of her brain. Stay tuned.